A World in Danger

DRIER

By Brenda McHale

PowerKiDS press
New York

Published in 2022 by The Rosen Publishing Group, Inc.
29 East 21st Street, New York, NY 10010

Edited by:
Madeline Tyler

Designed by:
Gareth Liddington

Cataloging-in-Publication Data

Names: McHale, Brenda.
Title: Drier / Brenda McHale.
Description: New York : PowerKids Press, 2022. | Series: A world in danger | Includes glossary and index.
Identifiers: ISBN 9781725335974 (pbk.) | ISBN 9781725335998 (library bound) | ISBN 9781725335981 (6 pack) | ISBN 9781725336001 (ebook)
Subjects: LCSH: Droughts--Juvenile literature. | Climatic changes--Effect of human beings on--Juvenile literature. | Climate change mitigation--Juvenile literature.
Classification: LCC QC929.25 M343 2022 | DDC 551.57'73--dc23

Manufactured in the United States of America

CPSIA Compliance Information: Batch #CWPK22.
For Further Information contact Rosen Publishing, New York, New York at 1-800-237-9932.

PHOTO CREDITS

Cover & Throughout – Studio-360, edella, passion artist, Milan M, Perfect Lazybones, 2– Juice Flair, 4&5 – Roofsoldier, SNEHIT PHOTO, 6&7 – Minko Peev, Gino Santa Maria, 8&9 – AustralianCamera, hilmawan nurhatmadi, 10&11 – Piyaset, arhendrix, 12&13 – STOCK'BURIN, Ares Jonekson, R_Tee, 14&15 – NASA, Lovisa Selander, 16&17 – Adriana Mahdalova, Vlad Karavaev, 18&19 – apple 2499, LCAT Productions, 20&21 – Halfpoint, Ricardo Mayer, 22&23 – Olesia Bilkei, Polina Yanchuk.

Images are courtesy of Shutterstock.com. With thanks to Getty Images, Thinkstock Photo and iStockphoto.

CONTENTS

Words that look like this can be found in the glossary on page 24.

ARE WEATHER AND CLIMATE DIFFERENT?

Weather changes every day and sometimes even a few times in a day. Rain, snow, and sunshine are all different kinds of weather.

The climate is the usual weather a place has for a very long time. There are different types of climate.

An arid climate is dry and hot.

WHAT IS CLIMATE CHANGE?

Climates have always changed very slowly, but now they are changing much faster. Many places in the world are getting warmer. Some places are getting drier, wetter, or windier. This is climate change.

Dry areas may get drier with climate change!

The way people are living is putting lots of gases into the atmosphere around Earth. This traps heat from the sun around Earth. As Earth gets hotter, it gets drier too.

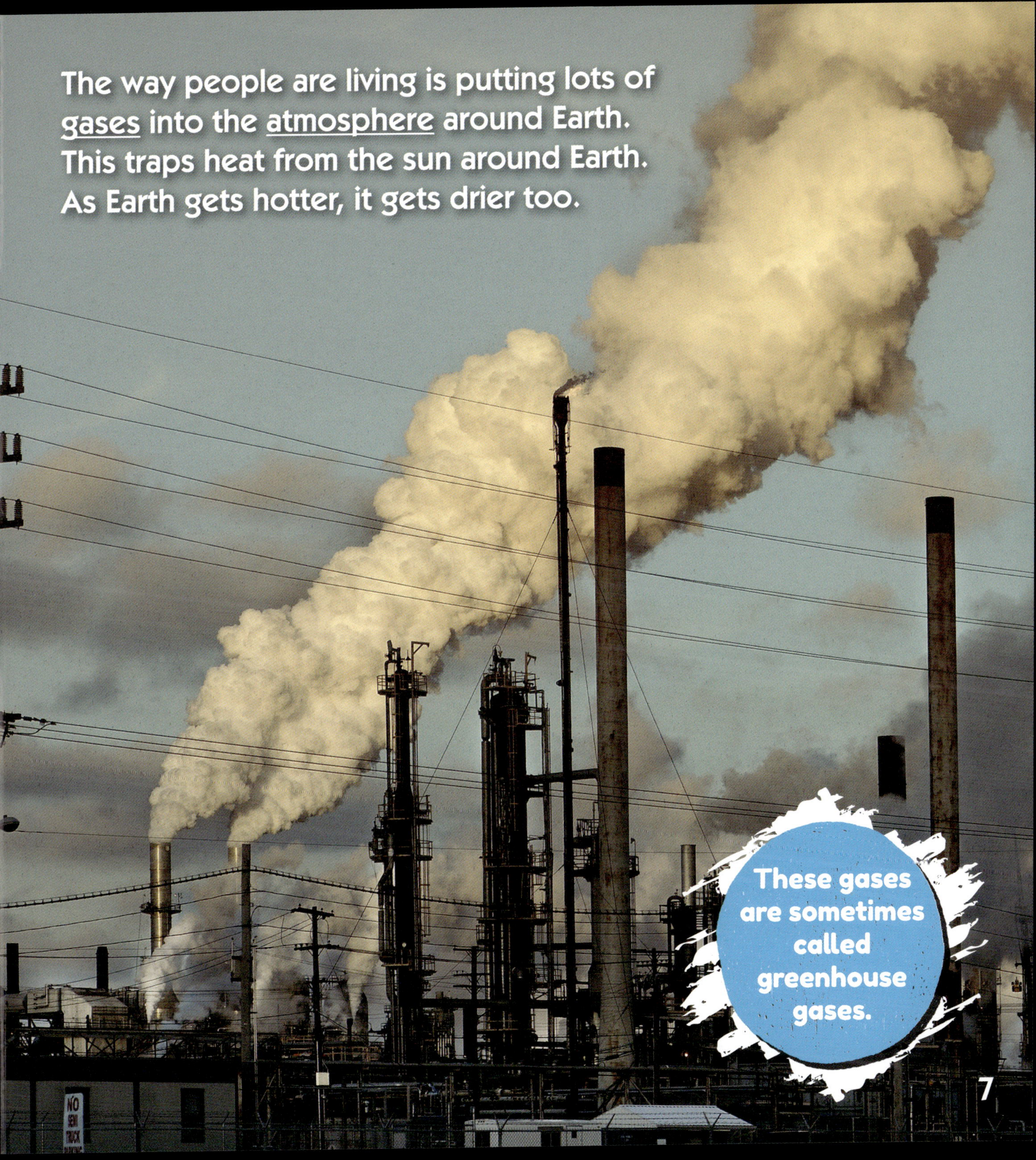

These gases are sometimes called greenhouse gases.

WHY ARE TREES IMPORTANT?

Carbon dioxide is one of the gases people are putting into the atmosphere. Trees absorb carbon dioxide. Their roots keep soil in place and hold water. They also provide homes for many animals.

Humans chop trees down to clear land for farming. This is called deforestation. When lots of trees get chopped down, it leaves more carbon dioxide in the atmosphere, and the soil can get very dry.

WHAT IS A DROUGHT?

A drought is when there has not been enough rain for a long time. Droughts can last for weeks, months, or even years. Some places, called deserts, never get much rain.

Droughts can mean that food crops don't grow. Animals may die because there is not enough food to eat and no fresh water to drink.

WHY DO DROUGHTS HAPPEN?

Warm air makes water evaporate from the ground, rivers, and seas. The water vapor forms clouds. When the clouds get too heavy, the water falls as rain. It then evaporates and makes clouds again.

As the Earth is getting warmer and climates are changing, there is less rain in some places. This means these places are having more droughts.

Fires can start more easily.

Drinking water can dry up.

LAKE POOPÓ, BOLIVIA

Lake Poopó is in Bolivia in South America. It used to be the country's second-largest lake but by the end of 2015, it had completely dried up. All that is left now is salt from the water.

People used to catch fish in the lake to eat and sell. No water means there are no fish. This has meant that many people have moved away, and others have had to try to build farms.

KENYA

Kenya is in Africa. It has an arid climate. During droughts, there is not enough food for people because crops die. Animals don't get enough to drink, so they can't make milk.

People are learning to grow different crops that can survive droughts better. When a drought comes, the people living there sometimes move to another area. They take their animals with them too.

AUSTRALIAN ANIMALS

Koalas eat mainly eucalyptus leaves. Australia is getting drier and having more fires. Forest fires burn down the eucalyptus trees and the koalas go hungry. Koalas can be hurt in bad fires too.

Scientists think temperatures in Australia will rise about two degrees Celsius by 2030. There will be less water, and this will put many animals, such as kangaroos, in danger.

IS IT TOO LATE TO STOP CLIMATE CHANGE?

You can tell other people what you have learned.

Earth's climate is changing faster than ever. By making changes and telling other people what they can do to help, we can slow climate change and make a difference.

People now know more about climate change. They are telling world leaders that they need to make rules to protect the planet.

You could write a letter to your government to tell them about climate change.

WHAT CAN WE DO TO HELP?

Put on a sweater or slippers if you're cold. This will use less heat so that fewer gases are put into the atmosphere.

You could ask your grown-up if you can have some of your meals without meat. If people eat less meat, farmers won't need to cut down trees to make room for more farm animals.

This veggie burger looks good!

GLOSSARY

absorb to take in or soak up

atmosphere the mixture of gases that make up the air and surround Earth

crops plants that are grown on a large scale to be eaten or used

evaporate to turn from a liquid into a gas or vapor

gases matter, like air, that fills any space available

government the group of people who are in charge of a country and decide its laws

survive to continue to live

vapor tiny parts of a solid or liquid that float in the air as a gas, such as mist or steam

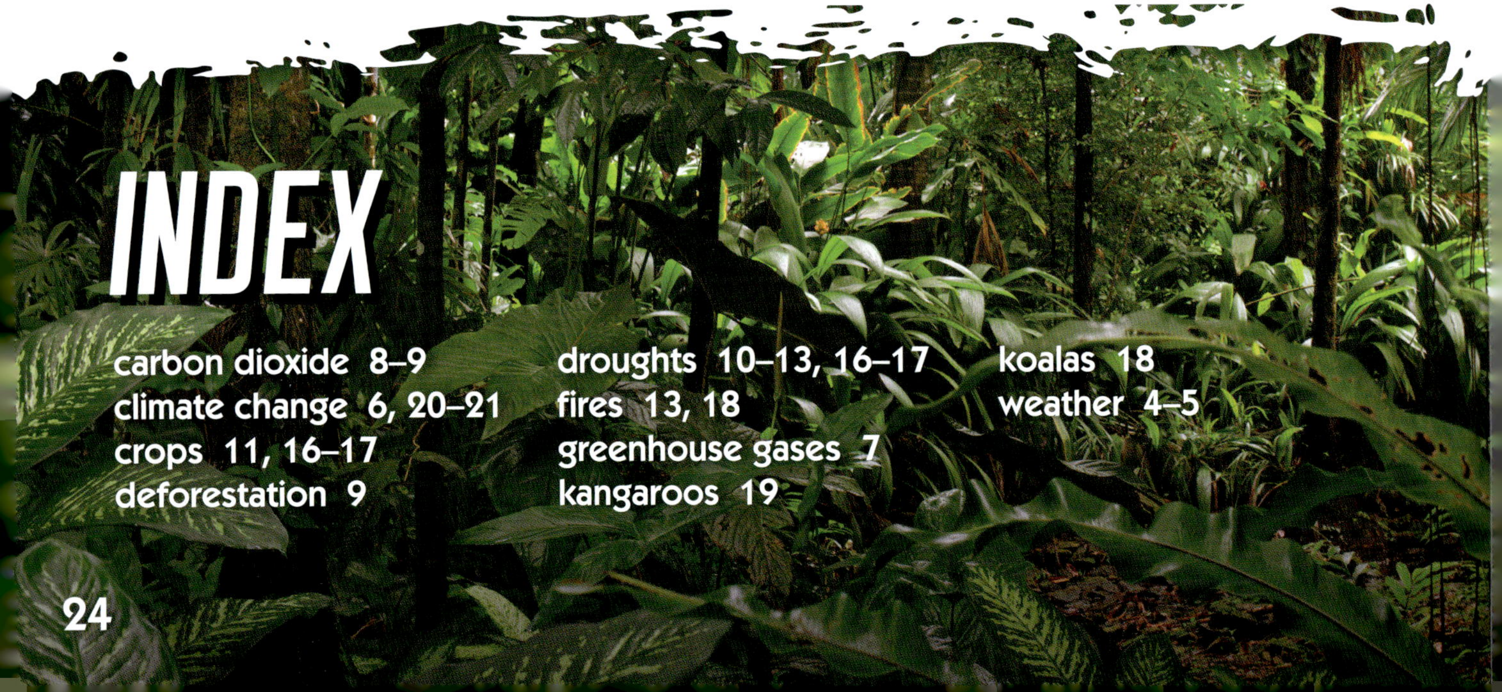

INDEX